Drive Right in France – from Calais to Marseilles

Lezli Rees

Laughing Dog Media
Warwickshire, UK

First published in February 2015 by Laughing Dog Media,
The Studio, 205 High Street, Henley-in-Arden,
Warwickshire B95 5BA.

ISBN 978-0-9927197-2-2

The contents of this book are believed correct at the time of publishing. Nevertheless neither the author nor the publisher can be held responsible for any errors or omissions or for changes in the details given in the book, or for the consequences of any reliance on the information it provides. This does not affect your statutory rights. We have tried to ensure accuracy in the book but things do change and we would be grateful if readers would advise us of any changes they may encounter at info@drivingwithdogs.co.uk

We have taken care to ensure that these walks are safe. The author or publisher cannot accept responsibility for any injuries caused to readers whilst following these walks.

British Library Cataloguing in Publication Data. A catalogue record for this book is available from the British Library.

Photographs and map by the author.

To the reader

Researching this book has been huge fun, and a real journey of discovery into parts of France that are often bypassed by motorway drivers.

Thanks are due to my long-suffering husband, David, who drove the campervan and maintained a stoic silence after each map-reading disaster. Our dog, Jem, deserves a mention for turning on his canine charm and facilitating conversations with people who might otherwise have driven us off their land with a pitchfork.

What we enjoyed most was the friendliness and welcoming spirit of the local residents. Most memorable moments included a trip out to the marshes near St Omer at the invitation of a boatman who wouldn't let us leave until we'd seen this special environment (and it was wonderful), learning to love fresh nougat near Orange – much better than wine tasting, an impromptu cookery lesson using wild herbs and leaves in a cafe in Provence, and right at the end of the trip Jem was 'spotted' in Martigues and appeared on local TV as part of a fashion show!

I hope you enjoy the walks as much as we did, and use this book to find adventures of your own.

Lezli Rees
January 2015

Contents

Where the walks are

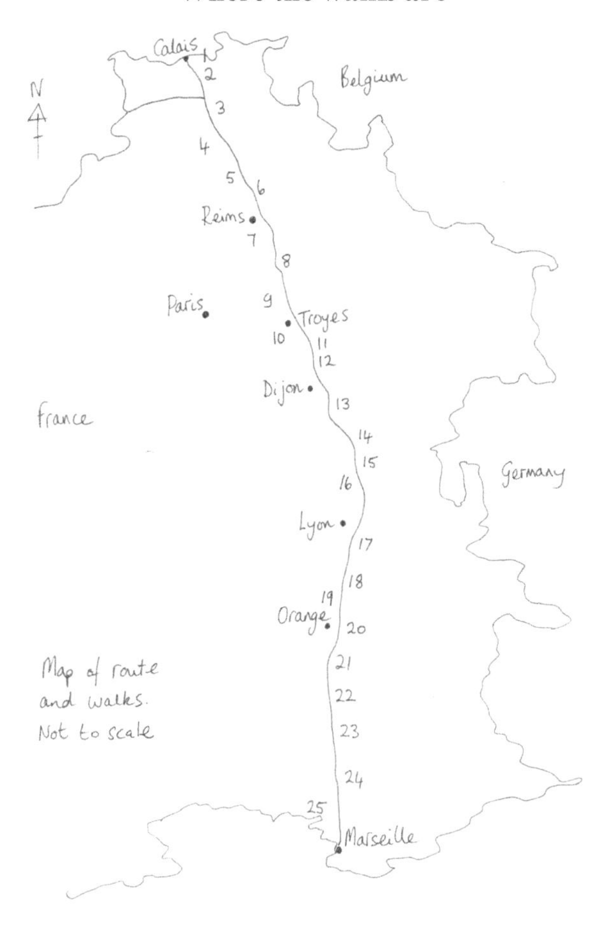

Introduction

This is a guide to some of France's hidden gems, all within 10km of motorway exits on the route from Calais to Marseilles.

The book will appeal to anyone driving to the South of France who wants to see more than the view from the motorway. I've chosen places to stop for a walk and a breather not just because they are easy to get to, but because they also meet the needs of families driving with kids, dogs or campervans. So you'll find a choice of little-visited and unspoiled towns and villages, forests, places with interesting historical connections and above all somewhere to experience different parts of France from the inside.

Twenty-five special places have been selected for this book. For each entry you'll find practical information, including GPS co-ordinates and detailed written directions for getting there, and back to the autoroute (motorway) again; where to buy picnic supplies and fuel; whether you can park a campervan; where to enjoy a short walk, children's activities, and what to see. Dog owners will find contact details of the nearest vet to each stop. All the walks are suitable for children.

The route

Calais is linked to Marseilles by around 1100km of motorways. You could do the whole drive in less than 10 hours, which isn't fun at all and makes most drivers a bit grumpy for a few days afterwards.

From Calais to Troyes the route takes the A26, also known as the '*autoroute des anglais*' because so much of the traffic is going to and from England. On motorway signs in France the A26 is also marked as the E15, which is the road's European number. You may be surprised to find that the E15 actually starts in Inverness and goes from there to Dover.

From Troyes, a timbered medieval town that gave us the traders' 'Troy' ounce, the route heads to Dijon and then takes the A39 to Lyon via Dole to avoid what is often a 70mph traffic jam of snorting HGVs on the parallel route on the A6.

Once past Lyon the A7 heads purposefully south to the Mediterranean, with town walks to be had at the Roman amphitheatre in Orange or in Cavaillon, the melon capital of France. More rural walks are to be found in sun-kissed lavender fields in pretty Provencale villages. Here you're driving on the '*autoroute soleil*' (sunshine highway), which is a cheerful experience for sun-starved Brits.

Autoroute driving tips

To comply with French driving law, you should equip yourself with a breathalyser, high-viz yellow jacket for at least the driver, fire extinguisher and a first-aid pack. These can be bought cheaply on-line before you go, although the breathalysers can be picked up in any French *pharmacie* (chemist) much cheaper than in the UK. The high-viz jackets are light and practical and available in all sizes, including small ones for kids. In the event of a breakdown you should wear your jackets, day or night. We have one for everyone in the car, and one for the dog as well.

Drivers are required to stop for a break every 2 hours. This law isn't enforceable, but is a sensible road safety measure. With this handy guide you'll find it easy to combine the 2-hour breaks with a mix of pit-stops and interesting places to visit.

Aires de repos

The *aires de repos* that appear every 20km or so on the French motorways always have WCs and picnic tables, easy parking for caravans and motorhomes and are a real bonus of the French motorway system.

For canine passengers, the quality of these rest places varies greatly. The main problem is that the entire motorway system is encased in mile after mile of high, very secure fencing. So although you may find a rest stop right in the middle of a forest there's no way you can get in there.

The WCs also vary in quality. Many have 'elephant feet' style WCs, healthy but not easy for everyone to manage. Tip: be prepared with your own supply of loo paper as this isn't always supplied.

Fuel and food are not available at *aires de repos*.

Aires de Service

These are the equivalent of motorway services, and provide food, fuel and WCs.

As in the UK, food here is usually over-priced and over-processed fast food. Fuel too is more expensive.

There is one exception, the Aire de Service de Jura (walk 17) is the best motorway services imaginable and certainly one of the finest in Europe.

Walking in France

France has an extensive system of long-distance footpaths. These are well-maintained and signed with wooden signposts, and some of the walks in this book use short sections of these routes. Rural paths are well-signed too, with path signs painted on to trees and gates.

A stroll in France is more than sightseeing, and you can expect cheery greetings from other walkers. Children and dogs are great ice-breakers and chance meetings can lead to experiences that become unexpected holiday highlights. Don't miss out!

Dog Etiquette

Without a language barrier, dogs from either side of the Channel will interact normally with each other. Any difficulties will often arise from the different dog training and socialisation habits of their accompanying people.

When walking in the forests most dogs will be off-lead. However, when another dog is spotted you can expect to see the owner put their dog on the lead immediately to avoid an off-lead encounter. If you see this happening, etiquette is to put your dog on the lead too.

Once dogs are safely on lead, do expect to be engaged in a doggie conversation – particularly if your pooch is a stylish breed.

Dogs are generally welcomed in cafés and restaurants with outside tables (not inside) and a large bucket of fresh dog water is nearly always provided for canine visitors. Don't be surprised if your waiter or other customers give your dog food treats, however improbable, without asking - this seems to be a conversation opener. Our dog gained a passion for French cuisine, but if your dog has a sensitive digestion the results of this random treating can be catastrophic.

And so onto dog poo. The picking-up rules are the same as in the UK and the supply of free bags is generous. Used bags can be dropped in the nearest general waste-bin.

The further south you go, the fewer restrictions there are on taking dogs into outdoor museums, formal gardens and other attractions. Never leave your dog in the car, the inside temperature heats rapidly and could prove fatal to your dog.

Useful websites to help you plan your trip

More walks for drivers in France:
www.motorwaybreaksfrance.co.uk

For dog owners

Pet passport regulations:
https://www.gov.uk/take-pet-abroad/overview
Dog walks, beaches and vet clinics in France:
www.drivingwithdogs.co.uk

1

A26 exit 2 - Les Hemmes de Marck

Before or after a channel crossing this enormous sandy beach and coast path is a great place to take in fresh air and sea breezes. Even at the height of summer it's rarely crowded, and children and dogs can run safely for miles.

Getting there

GPS: 50° 59' 12.8394" N 1° 57' 43.38" E
Distance from Calais: 9 km

From Calais Ferry Port

Leave the ferry port and then turn right at the first roundabout signed Oye-Plage, Marck. Drive over a level crossing and take the 2nd left turn onto Route de Gravelines (the sign says no left turn, but this is only for vehicles over 3.5 T). Continue for 4.8 km and take the left turn signed Les Hemmes de Marck. After 2 km, enter Les Hemmes de Marck and turn left just after a right turn to Oye Plage and a 45 km/hr speed limit sign. At the turning there is a very small street sign for Chemin de la Digue. Take this road and turn left to reach the free parking at the beach.

From Eurotunnel Terminal

Exit the Eurotunnel terminal and bear right at the fork to join the A16, signed Calais, Lille, Reims, Paris. Leave the A16 at junction 48 signed for Marck-Ouest. Turn left, this is the D247 Rue Pascal. Go through one roundabout. At the second roundabout take exit 2, D248, Avenue de Verdun. After 2 km turn right onto the D119 and after nearly 2 km turn left onto the

D119E1, Rue des Islandais. Carry on for 1 km and then turn right, Rue Robelin, and after 150m bear left to stay on Rue Robelin. This becomes the coast road, Chemin de la Digue. Follow this road when it bends right and turn left to reach the free parking at the beach.

Return to A26

Exit the dunes and turn right. Follow the road back to Les Hemmes de Marck and turn right at the T-junction. Continue ahead and at the T-junction with the D119, turn right signed Calais. After 350m turn left signed Marck Centre. Enter Marck and, at the roundabout with the windmill centrepiece, carry straight on signed A16-A26. Go straight on at the next roundabout, then bear right to merge with the A16. Stay on the A16 for 2.5 km, then take the turning signed A26 St Omer, Arras, Reims, Paris. Continue ahead, keeping in the right hand lane, to merge with the A26.

Walk

When the tide is out you'll find mile after mile of sandy beach, definitely a space for ball games and high octane rushing around.

At high tide the beach disappears, but a signed coastal path leads eastwards through the dunes above the high tide mark. After several miles you'll reach a bird reserve at Oye Plage and at migration time it's well worth taking binoculars with you to spot some of the thousands of birds taking a breather before heading north or south on their journey. It's possible to walk as far as the outskirts of Gravelines if you have several hours to spare.

Local info

Free parking. Campervan access.

Small outdoor café and WCs at a campsite on the track to the beach, open in summer.

Nearest fuel station: 24/7 fuel at Esso Nord, 361 Ave Antoine de St-Exupery, Calais.

Nearest vet: Clinique Vétérinaire Saint Antoine, 127 Rue Pascal, 62730 Marck. Tel: 03 21 46 53 53 (on the D131 towards Calais).

2A
A26 exit 2 - Forest of Éperlecques

The Forest of Éperlecques covers a vast area and it would take a lot of walking to exhaust the many trails here.

Getting there

GPS: 50° 49' 36.768" N 2° 10' 55.4664" E
10 km from A26 exit 2

Leave the A26 at junction 2 and take the D217, Éperlecques, Blockhaus d'Éperlecques. Turn right signed D943, St Omer, Blockhaus d'Éperlecques. Turn left signed D221, Bayenghem, Blockhaus d'Éperlecques. Continue straight ahead, driving through Le Mont, then pass the Château de Ganspette Campsite and turn left signed Blockhaus d'Éperlecques. Continue to reach the car parks, both are on the left and the forest car park is 50m before the entrance to the museum.

Return to A26 Junction 2

Turn right from the forest or museum car park and turn right at the T-junction. Continue straight to the next T-junction. Turn right, signed A26 and then turn left, signed A26. Follow signs to return to the A26.

Walk

An information board in the car park gives an overview of the forest trails and wildlife you may be able to spot. The trails are colour coded and vary in length from a 1.5km walk 'Chemin des Sorts', the 3km Chemin de

Saint Gilles and several others. One path is wheelchair accessible.

The trails aren't very clearly marked, but a pattern of 20 minutes heading rightwards, 20 minutes leftwards, and a final 20 minutes left again gave us a fabulous hour of circular walking. Dogs and children will adore the chance to hurtle around the woodland, while weary drivers may opt for the chance for a snooze under a tree in this tranquil and inviting woodland.

Paths are a mixture of clear forest tracks and footpaths.

The forest is within walking distance from the Blockhaus d' Éperlecques museum (see Walk 2B). Most visitors will be heading for the museum, and so you're likely to have the car park and forest to yourselves.

It's an ideal spot for a proper off-lead dog walk, and just the job for giving the hound a good run after his ferry ordeal - or on your return route.

Local info

Forest car park: cars only, free. No campervan access, but on-road parking is possible.

Nearest supermarkets: Vival and Carrefour supermarkets in Watten.

Fuel: Carrefour supermarket on the D207, Rue de bleue Maison.

Tourist Information office: 12, rue de Dunkerque, Watten.

Nearest vet: Dr Jean Paulus, 21 Rue de bleue Maison, Éperlecques (at the D207/D300 junction). Tel: 03 21 88 46 00.

2B

A26 exit 2 - Blockhaus d'Éperlecques

Just a short way from the forest car park is the entrance to the extraordinary (and dog-friendly) outdoor museum of the Bunker of Éperlecques. During World War Two conscripts and prisoners were forced to build a mammoth facility intended to launch powerful V-2 rockets across the channel towards London. Fortunately the site didn't become operational, thanks to some sturdy sabotage work by the workforce. Today it's a sombre but fascinating place and of all the many military installations in the region now on show as 'heritage sites' on the tourist trail, we rated the information and visitor facilities here highly.

Getting there

GPS: 50° 49' 36.768" N 2° 10' 55.4664" E
10.4 km from A26

From junction 2 take the D217, Eperlecques, Blockhaus d'Eperlecques. Turn right signed D943, St Omer, Blockhaus d'Eperlecques. Turn left signed D221, Bayenghem, Blockhaus d'Eperlecques. Continue straight ahead, driving through Le Mont, then pass the château de Ganspette Campsite and turn left signed Blockhaus d'Eperlecques. Continue to reach the museum car park on the left and 50m after a forest car park.

Return to A26 Junction 2

Turn right out of the car park and turn right at the T-junction. Continue straight to the next T-junction. Turn right, signed A26 and then turn left, signed A26. Continue following the signs to return to the A26.

Walk

The outdoor museum is a popular attraction for anyone interested in military history, however remotely. And the glory of this museum is that it's surrounded by an enormous forest with loads of footpaths to give everyone a leg stretch.

The museum is the Blockhaus d' Éperlecques, a concrete monolith built by slave labour in WW2 so that V2 rockets could be launched towards London. Fortunately, thanks to the combined efforts of the RAF and successful sabotage on the ground, this particular Nazi effort was thwarted.

Even if military history isn't your thing, the museum is definitely interesting. Dogs on leads are allowed to go with you around the self-guided circular route with no restrictions.

Nearly all the tour is on hard surfaced paths that wind through attractive woodland, and are easy for buggies and wheelchairs.

An hour is probably the shortest time to see everything, and it would be easy to spend longer here.

Local info

Museum car park: free, with zoned campervan and caravan parking. www.leblockhaus.com/en/

Museum: entry charge. Opening times: March 1100-1700, April and October 1000-1800, May-September 1000-1900, November 1415-1700. Closed 1 December-28 February.

WC+disabled inside museum.

Wheelchair access to museum, largely firm paths and concrete.

Refreshments: Small café/snack bar (open 1200-1430 mid-June – mid September) small selection of snacks, chocolate bars and hot/cold drinks.

Children's discovery activities.

Nearest supermarkets: Vival and Carrefour supermarkets in Watten.

Fuel: Carrefour supermarket on the D207, Rue de bleue Maison, Watten.

Tourist Information office: 12, rue de Dunkerque, Watten.

Nearest vet: Jean Paulus, 21 rue Bleue Maison, Eperlecques (GPS: 50° 49' 18.1194" N 2° 11' 55.7154" E). Tel: 03 21 88 46 00 (2.1 km).

3

A26 Junction 3
St Omer, Jardin Public

The quaint town of St Omer with its celebrated gothic-style cathedral, elegant Flanders town houses and thriving market is an ideal place for a first (or last) night in France.

Getting there

GPS: 50° 44' 52.5546" N 2° 14' 57.8466" E
8.8 km from A26

From A26 Junction 3 take exit 3 at the roundabout, signed D942, Calais, St Omer. Stay in the right hand lane and continue, signed St Omer, Lille. Continue on the D942 and take exit 2 at the next roundabout, D928, St Omer. At the next roundabout take exit 1, signed St Omer, to continue on the D928. At the following roundabout, take exit 3, signed D928, St Omer-Centre Ville. Carry straight on at the next roundabout (Toutes Directions) and at the following roundabout take exit 1, signed A26, Autre Directions. Go straight at the next roundabout and then turn right at the final roundabout on Boulevard Vauban to reach the car park.

Return to A26 Junction 3

Exit the car park and turn right onto Boulevard Vauban. Continue ahead, Toutes Directions, and at the next roundabout take exit 1, signed A26 Reims. At the following roundabout, take exit 1 signed A26, Toutes Directions, D928, then turn left signed Calais A26. At the roundabout take exit 3 signed D942, Calais and continue as signed to return to the A26.

Walk

Saint Omer is famous for its beer, and all around the central square you'll find convivial bars and cafes that are great for a bit of people watching. You may also find your eyes drawn to the high, very sloping roofs of the buildings and wonder if you've somehow strayed into Belgium by mistake.

The town has been considerably squabbled over in its history. The massive city walls you can see from the park are just part of the defences ordered by Louis 14th in his bid to snatch St Omer from the Spanish and grab the town for France. The walls are still very impressive.

To get into the 20 acre park, return to the main road from the parking space and turn left. Walk about 25 meters to a gate, and the path here will lead you into the formal gardens. Cut across these to the far right hand corner, and then you'll be on a firm path leading into woodland.

Once underway, most paths lead towards a small domestic animal zoo, with a collection of sociable goats, deer and poultry. Two play areas for young and older children are close to the zoo.

There's no fixed route here - the park is just the right size for a gentle amble without worrying about getting lost.

Local info

Free parking. WCs opposite park entrance. Plenty of cafés, crêperies and shops for picnic provisions in the town.

Carrefour supermarket with fuel station signed on the way into St Omer on D928 from the motorway.

Tourist Information Office to the right of the WCs opposite the park entrance.

www.tourisme-saintomer.com/gb/home.htm

Market day: Wednesday morning

Nearest vet: Clinique Vétérinaire des Docteurs Gerion et Dandrifosse, 5 Rue de Belfort, Saint Omer (GPS: 50 45' 20.88" N 2° 15' 34.956" E). Tel: 03 21 88 87 54.

4

A26 Junction 8 - Bourlon Forest

Bourlon is a small village cradled by calm and tranquil woodland. You'll see the impeccably tended Canadian war memorial to soldiers slain in World War 1 during action to take control of Bourlon Hill in the final stages of the war.

Getting there

GPS: 50° 10' 26.889" N 3° 7' 4.9296" E
6.2 km from A26

From junction 8 take the D939, Cambrai. Take the 1st right, D340 Bourlon. Continue through the village, almost to the end. Pass one sign to the Canadian military cemetery. Turn left when signed to Canadian Monument. Drive to the small shaded car park on a quiet residential street at the base of the memorial steps.

Return to A26 Junction 8

Turn round and return to the village - there's a one way system which will stop you from going straight down the hill. At the end of the one-way section, turn right onto the major road and then carry on through the village and back to the D939. Turn left and then rejoin the A26 as signed.

Walk

This walk starts at the Canadian memorial and then follows a woodland path where dogs are able to run off lead. You're likely to have the walk to yourselves as this is a quiet and sleepy area.

At first glance there doesn't seem to be much of a walk here, as the immaculately kept memorial to Canadian soldiers dominates the parking area. It's beautifully maintained, and lies between an impressive avenue of lime trees. These trees were shattered during WW1 and have been restored to health over decades of careful tending.

Take the path which starts to the left of the memorial slope (as you look at it) and walk past another memorial, this time to members of the French Resistance. Keep the memorial with its distinctive Cross of Lorraine to your right, and continue along the shaded woodland path as far as a small Canadian cemetery which will be on your left.

Turn right here, where a less trodden but clear path leads into the forest. This is ideal for off-lead dog scampering and there's plenty of space and paths to keep you walking for quite a while.

We went to the end of the path, and then turned right in a clearing before turning round and following the route in reverse back to the car park. This gives a 30-40 minute walk.

Local info

Free parking. Campervan access.

Small café/bars in Bourlon, pâtisserie, boulangerie, chemist.

Nearest vet: 7 Rue du Calvaire, Inchy en Artois (GPS: 50° 10' 36.1194" N 3° 2' 58.74" E). Tel: 03 21 59 53 87 (6.5 km).

5

A26 Junction 9 - Vaucelles Abbey Park and the St Quentin Canal

Three varied walks can be found here. Keen gardeners will relish the chance to have a look at the specialist gardens surrounding the site of a former Cistercian monastery, and a longer leg-stretch also starts from the monastery car park. A stroll on the canal towpath is ideal for buggies/wheelchairs and if you're lucky you'll see large commercial barges at work.

Getting there

GPS: 50° 4' 34.7952" N 3° 13' 17.1834" E (Abbey car park)
5.1 km from A26

From junction 9 turn right, D917, Bonavis. At Bonavis bear right and then immediately turn right before the Bonavis Grill Restaurant. Follow the road round over two bridges, round a bend, and the large abbey car park is immediately on the left.

For the canal walk, turn right after the second bridge and park by the picnic tables.

Return to A26 Junction 9

Turn right out of the car park and retrace the route to Bonavis. Turn left and continue ahead following the signs to return to the A26.

Walks

Walk 1 - The Cistercian Abbey of Vaucelles

If you're a gardening enthusiast, this is the walk to aim for. As long as you plan to arrive while the Abbey gardens are open to the public. Opening times are: mid-March to October 31st, Tuesday to Saturday 1000-1200 and 1400-1730; Sunday 1500-1830. Entry charge, children free, dogs on leads. Details: www.abbayedevaucelles.com

Vaucelles Abbey dates from the 12th century and in its day boasted the biggest chapter house in Europe. The French Revolution saw the abbey shut down, and many of its walls demolished to be re-used for domestic buildings. German occupation in WW1 put what was left of the abbey in the middle of fierce fighting and the library and church were gutted by fire. So until recently there hasn't been much to see.

Restoration work to the abbey and gardens is on-going. One hall is now used for concerts and several varieties of boxwood form part of the garden restoration. There are guided tours through the buildings, but the hours are quite limited.

Walk 2

This is an ideal walk if you're waiting for the abbey to open, and gives more boisterous passengers the chance to let off steam before going in to see the gardens.

The car parking is still in the abbey car park, and you just walk back along the road to the tight corner and turn left at the footpath sign to 'les Hauts du Cambrésis' (it's a UK-style wooden post). The path is wide and leafy and will take you gently up a hill. This is part of a much longer walk so there's plenty of scope for a walk as long as you like.

Walk 3 - Canal de St Quentin, Circuit des Mérovingiens

The Canal de St Quentin was constructed in the early 1800s and was once the main trading thoroughfare between Belgium and Paris. It was so busy that work was constantly ongoing to strengthen the banks and locks. With the opening of the bigger Canal du Nord in

1965 as a replacement route, the St Quentin is now a quieter waterway and very pleasant for a stroll. You may well see commercial traffic on it still, and the lock chambers and machinery are impressive.

The full route of the signed Circuit des Mérovingiens is a 15km hike and takes in several historic sites, including a Carolingian chapel and a Mérovingian necropolis. It's too long for a motorway break, but the easy section along the towpath is worthwhile.

Local info

Canal: Free parking. Campervan access. Picnic tables. No facilities.

Abbey: Free parking. Campervan access. WC when abbey is open. The Bonavis Grill restaurant is on the corner just before the turn to Vaucelles.

Tourist Information: http://en.tourisme-cambresis.fr

Nearest vet: Clinique Vétérinaire Saint Antoine, 32 Rue d'Hermenne, Proville (GPS: 50° 8' 42" N 3° 12' 40.428" E). Tel: 03 27 82 79 70 (10.4 km).

6

A26 Junction 10 - St Quentin and the Marais d'Isle Nature Reserve

The story of St Quentin is largely that of a town founded by the Romans on a strategically desirable spot on the banks of the Somme, followed by regular sackings and destruction thereafter. It became part of the Hindenburg Line in World War 1, when the population was forced to flee and nearly all the buildings were destroyed or badly damaged. The town we see today is a triumph of reconstruction, and the Basilica is well worth a visit.

Getting there

GPS: 49° 50' 55.7874" N 3° 17' 33.792" E
5.6 km from A26

From junction 10 keep in the left hand lane, signed St Quentin. Merge with the D1029 and continue ahead towards St Quentin, carrying straight on at two roundabouts. On approaching a 3rd roundabout, take the left filter lane and turn left (unsigned). Continue straight on for 900m and at a crossroads turn left, signed Cambrai, Palais des Sports. Carry straight on at the 1st roundabout, then take exit 2 at the 2nd roundabout, signed Palais des Sports. After 180m turn right and park beside the city park.

Note: there's a comprehensive one-way system in the town.

Return to A26 Junction 10

Continue straight ahead and follow the road to the right as it merges onto Boulevard Gambetta (signed Gendarmerie). At the roundabout, take exit 2 signed Le Splendid, then take the 1st right turn. At the crossroads turn left and carry straight on. Turn right at the T-junction, signed Résidence Victor Hugo and after 700m follow the blue autoroute signs at the traffic light controlled junction. Merge onto the dual carriageway and carry straight on following the blue autoroute signs to return to the A26.

Walk

A stroll and nose around the town will take longer than 30 minutes, but if you're over-nighting here, or just want to see more, a visit to the UNESCO Marais d'Isle nature reserve shows a completely different aspect of the town.

You could walk there from the centre, but it's a lot easier to drive across the canal bridge (N2029) and access the paths directly. GPS: 49.849080, 3.311434.

The reserve is very watery and is a combination of the St Quentin canal towpath and the floodplain of the River Somme, managed now to provide wildlife habitat, and watersports facilities. Firm paths run along the river bank and discovery trail leaflets are available from the Maison de l'Environnement at the entrance to the park. It is a completely unique environment, and very calming.

Local info

P&D metered parking in town. Campervan access. Public WC near the basilica. Plenty of shops, cafés and restaurants with outdoor seating in the town.

TOTAL fuel station on dual carriageway (return route).

Tourist Information:
http://www.saint-quentin-tourism.co.uk

Market day: Wednesday and Saturday mornings in the town centre.

Nearest vet: Dr Daniel Carton, 7 Rue Wager, Saint Quentin (GPS: 49° 50' 36.24" N 3° 17' 35.484" E). Tel: 03 23 62 09 85.

7

A26 Junction 13 - Laon

Perched on a hilltop with wide ranging views over the countryside, the medieval town of Laon has been a place of refuge, a strategic target and a landmark of the region for many centuries. Its famed Gothic cathedral attracts visitors year round, and the surrounding cobbled streets make exploring a delight.

Getting there

GPS: 49° 33' 52.92" N 3° 37' 13.764" E
9.4 km from A26

From junction 13 take exit 1 at the roundabout, N2 Laon. Continue ahead on the N2 for 4.5 km, over 2 roundabouts, signed Laon. At the 3rd roundabout, take exit 1, D181, Laon Centre. Continue ahead over another 2 roundabouts (the 1st signed Laon Centre, the 2nd Centre Ville) and at the next roundabout take exit 2 signed Centre Ville. Turn left at the next roundabout, signed Chambry, Guise, then take exit 1 at the next roundabout. Continue ahead uphill, keeping left when the road forks under the elevated tramway to reach the medieval city. Turn left when signed for Cathédrale, Office du Tourisme, and continue ahead to reach the parking area in the square on the left hand side.

Return to A26 Junction 13

Turn right out of the parking area, then right again signed Toutes Directions. Go straight ahead to start driving down the hill. At the roundabout, take exit 3,

A26. The route back to the A26 is fully signed from this point, keep following the blue autoroute signs.

Walk

Not the obvious place to walk the dog perhaps, but this is a lovely place to stop to enjoy a relaxing meal or snack in the partly pedestrianised Old Town and take in the medieval atmosphere.

The ramparts walk starts from the coach parking area, which is just below (and easily seen from) the car park on the far side of the town as detailed in the directions.

Walk away from the town on the pedestrianised walkway that winds down the hill. This is more of a stroll to attend to doggy comfort, as the town itself will probably be the point of your stop here. Don't go too far, as it's a steep climb up again!

Then return to the car park to approach the town from the less touristy side, and enjoy a meander through the tiny medieval lanes and alleys, heading generally towards the cathedral. There are plenty of signs to the cathedral, but you're bound to make your own discoveries of seemingly forgotten haunts of the

Knights Templar and hidden sanctuaries of many other religious groups too.

Local info

P&D parking. Campervan access. Refreshments:The square and surrounding streets in front of the cathedral are full of restaurants and cafés. Nearly all of them have outside seating where dogs are welcome to sit with you.

Shops for picnic supplies and less touristic cafes are in the modern town at the foot of the hill.

TOTAL fuel station on D181, Avenue Charles de Gaulle, Laon.

Tourist Information: http://www.laon-tourism.co.uk

Nearest vet: Clinique Vétérinaire des Epinettes, 118 Avenue Pierre Mendès France, Laon (GPS: 49° 34' 46.5594" N 3° 38' 31.848" E). Tel: 03 23 23 37 47.

8

A26 Junction 14 - Canal latéral à l´Aisne, Berry au Bac

Although it's little more than a village, the name of Berry au Bac entered the history books as a key location of the First Battle of the Aisne in September 1914 at the start of World War 1, and marks the spot where trench warfare first began. The French 5th army crossed the river Aisne at Berry-au-Bac in an attempt to drive out the German army on the ridge beyond. Today it's just a small village with a well-stocked boulangerie.

Getting there

49° 23' 53.8002" N 3° 54' 7.9806" E
6 km from A26

From junction 14 follow signs for D925, Berry au Bac, turning left (exit 3) at the roundabout ornamented with a tank onto the N44 signed Reims, Berry au Bac.

Go through Berry au Bac village, and over two consecutive bridges marked 1 L'Aisne and 2 Canal Lateral l'Aisne. Turn immediately left onto a minor road/track straight after the second bridge. Straight away turn into the parking space on the grassy area opposite a set of recycling bins.

Return to A26 Junction 14

Exit the grassy area and turn right onto the road to return over the bridges and through the village. At the tank roundabout, take exit 1 signed A26. Continue following the blue signs to return to the A26.

Walk

If you're a canal fan, then this walk is full of interest and dogs will love it too. It's a towpath walk alongside a stretch of the Aisne canal and just fabulous! Nothing to do with walking - but if you've ever thought of living on a narrowboat, check out the sturdy large craft on view here first.

From the grassy parking space, walk back across the bridge over the canal and down onto the towpath on the other side by the lock-keeper's house. Don't be tempted to nip across the canal over the lock gates. These are fully automatic and open well in advance of approaching craft so you can't tell if it's safe or not, and the lock-keeper is ferocious.

The walk is then a pleasant and interesting stroll alongside the canal, with the chance to watch commercial barges (*peniches*) plying their trade. The canal runs parallel to the River Aisne and is a 51km link providing a east-west route via Reims to Conde-sur-Marne.

For a 40 minute walk, you're limited to 20 minutes each way - which seems to speed by.

Dogs are fine off-lead here, provided they can be trusted not to leap into the canal.

On your return drive to the A26, look out for the tank memorial by the roundabout just out of town. The monument marks the spot where France's first ever tanks entered battle in 1917. Sadly, most of the tanks were destroyed in their first offensive with heavy loss of life. A memorial service takes place here in April each year. The light tanks on the memorial date from the1950's.

Local info

Free parking. Campervan access.

Pizzeria in the village, on the right as you enter. Also a couple of cafés and a boulangerie for picnic supplies. Before you get to the parking spot for the walk there's a very handy car park on the left (entering Berry au Bac) in the middle of the village and if you are getting picnic stuff you'll save a short road walk by stopping here and then carrying on to the canal.

Nearest vet: Annabelle Rousseau, 6 Avenue du Général de Gaulle, Guignicourt (GPS: 49° 26' 4.56" N 3° 57' 56.304" E). Tel: 03 23 25 60 26 (8.3 km).

9

A26 Junction 17 - Faux de Verzy

The gnarled and curiously shaped trees of the Faux de Verzy are extraordinary, and will fascinate people of all ages. This walk is a longer drive from the A26, but absolutely worth it if you have the time for a 40-60 minute walk.

Getting there

GPS: 49° 8' 6.36" N 4° 9' 5.436" E
26.7 km from A26

From junction 17 take exit 3 at the roundabout, D3, Epernay. Continue for 8.5 km. Enter Jalons and turn right at the crossroads, D37, Rue de la Mairie. Follow the D37 as it bears round to the right and over a level crossing. Carry on between a series of lakes and at a roundabout take exit 3, signed D1, Tours s/M, Ay. Immediately take the right fork signed D34, Bouzy, and continue for 7.5 km. Enter Louvois and take the right fork signed Verzy. Continue straight on for 5.2 km and park in the Parc des Pins car park on the right.

Disabled access is easier from the Parc des Faux - a short distance from Parc des Pins on the same road.

The forest is within 20 miles of the A26 Junction 17 - so well outside the distance we'd normally suggest for a 'motorway walk'. If you have time to spare, though, then the forest is a delight and you could have a typically long and relaxed Gallic picnic.

Return to A26 Junction 17

Exit the car park and turn left. Return to Louvois and turn left onto the D34. Go straight on at the 1st roundabout, and turn right at the 2nd roundabout, signed Jalons. Enter Jalons and after going over the level crossing follow the road round to the left signed D37, Champigneul. At the crossroads, turn left signed A4 A26, and continue to follow the blue autoroute signs to return to the A26.

Walk

A lovely walk on well-signed paths through one of the curiosities of the forest. The cause of the peculiar gnarled and contorted beech trees of Verzy continues to baffle scientists, and they certainly make an interesting conversation topic for the walk.

The walk we chose here is a 45 minute circular walk through the groves of the weirdly shaped beech trees for which the forest is famous.

Starting from the interpretation board in the Park des Pins car park, a well signed and easy to follow trail winds comfortably through the shade of the trees with no steep gradients or stiles. This trail will take you close to the contorted and gnarly beeches, and have

keen gardeners scratching their heads for a solutio
these odd shapes. Scientists don't know the answe
either, although local legend has it that the effects followed a mighty curse on the non-believers of Verzy by either God, St Basil, or both.

Local info

Free car parks, all with campervan access. Picnic tables. Interpretation boards describing the special trees, wildlife and conservation strategy of the forest. Picnic supplies available from shops in Verzy.

There are no WCs in the forest; local practice is to nip behind a tree.

Nearest vet: Pascal Warez, 55 Rue Colbert, Taissy (49° 12' 55.44" N 4° 5' 10.716" E). Tel: 03 26 05 05 30 (13.9 km).

3 - Troyes

The medieval old town of Troyes in the Champagne region is well worth a visit, and a complete antidote to motorway driving. Its characteristic half-timbered buildings (and these are the originals as Troyes escaped the ravages of war), waterside walkway and attractive shops and restaurants are a delight.

The Tourism Office initiated France's first 'Toutourisme' section, especially for dogs and their owners. Take your Toutou there for a free doggy bag of useful gifts and info.

Getting there

GPS: 48° 17' 53.7" N 4° 4' 43.2834" E
8 km from A26

From junction 23 take exit 2 at the roundabout, signed Troyes, St Dizier. Continue for 5.7 km, continuing straight on through 4 roundabouts to follow the D619. On reaching the traffic light controlled junction, turn left, signed Centre Ville. At the traffic lights just before the river, turn right signed Troyes-Barberey and continue for 1 km. At the T-junction turn left, A5, and continue for 450m (a canal is on the left) to reach a parking area on the right hand side.

Return to A26 Junction 23

From the parking area, follow the sign for the A26 (on the opposite side of the canal, returning the way you came). After 400m turn right, signed Chaumont, Nancy and continue for 1 km (the river will be on the right). At the traffic lights by a bridge on the right, turn left and after 400m bear right at the lights, signed A5 Lyon, Toutes Directions, and continue to rejoin the A26.

Walk

The highlight of any visit to Troyes has to be to admire the fabulous half-timbered 16th century buildings of the old town and the cathedral roof in particular. The town was the provincial capital of the Champagne region for a long time, and the wealth of fine buildings reflects this status. A hint of the former importance of Troyes as a centre of trade and commerce is that the 'troy ounce' weight is named after the town.

We started at an intersection of the canal walkway right next to the house where Joan of Arc was once a resident (Rue Boucherat). The tower on the road side gives an insight into Troyes' medieval history, with only a couple of archer-proof windows visible from the outside.

Opposite this very famous house is a small park that seems to be popular with the town's dog walkers. There don't seem to be any restrictions on dogs in shops and cafés in the old town - we saw dogs everywhere.

A free guided tour app of the town can be downloaded to your iPhone from the App Store, or from Google Play. It's in English.

Local info

On street parking, mainly P&D.

Refreshments: Plenty of shops and little bistros, reasonably priced cafés and restaurants in the Old Town.

Touristic attractions which can be enjoyed from the outside - such as the medieval cathedral, a residence of Joan of Arc, lots of narrow streets with medieval timbered houses,

Shell fuel station on the D619, Avenue Robert Schumann.

Market day: Gastronomic market 'Les Matinées Gourmandes' on the first Wednesday of every month. Daily food market in the covered Halles, Rue de la République.

Tourist Office: 16, rue Aristide Briand, Troyes. Open Mon-Sat 0930-1830 May 1 to 15 September. Sept 16 to May 1: 0930-1230; 1400-1800. http://en.tourisme-troyes.com

Office du Toutouisme: welcome pack for dogs, with city dog guide and gifts. Inside Tourist Office.

Nearest vet: Dr Henri Longchamp, 22 Rue Jaillant Deschainets, Troyes (GPS: 48° 17' 47.0394" N 4° 4' 6.1314" E). Tel: 03 25 73 14 93.

11
A26 (E17) Junction 23 - Lac d’Orient

What an amazing place this is. A series of enormous lakes devoted to leisure facilities of all kinds, not just water sports. The lakes are artificial but the timber-framed farmhouses in the villages bordering the water are genuinely old.

Getting there

GPS: 48° 15' 52.2174" N 4° 17' 50.2836" E
12 km from A26

From junction 23 turn left at the roundabout (exit 4) signed D619, Lusigny-sur-Barse, Lac d'Orient. Turn left when signed to Lusigny-sur-Barse / Plage. Follow this road (Route du lac) as far as a signed car park on the left.

Return to A26 Junction 23

Turn right out of the car park and back into Lusigny. Go through the village and turn right onto the D619, and then re-join the motorway as signed.

Walk

You'd never guess, but these lakes are part of the River Seine flow management system, and in places you can see the 'river' apparently flowing in two completely different directions.

We headed for a beach, hoping to get Jem in for a swim. The beach was out of bounds for dogs, but a delight for kids. It's a good place for a fresh-water swim and you'll find a kiosk selling snacks and drinks in season.

A series of pathways is set aside for dog-walkers, and there's also a forest walk that's signed from the far end of the car park. The route of the woodland walk is marked with horizontal white and yellow footpath signs. You'll notice these painted onto trees at eye level. The path winds its way through the woods, and is a safe place to let dogs with good recall off the lead. We saw quite a few red squirrels here, which was a lovely surprise. The route is easy to follow, and for a 45 minute stroll you just follow the footpath marks for 20 minutes or so and then turn to reverse your tracks back to the car park.

Local info

At the car park: free parking, seasonal snack bar, WC, campervan access, picnic tables.

In Lusigny-sur-Barse: free parking, pâtisserie, boulangerie, chemist.

TOTAL fuel station on D619, Avenue Pierre Gomand, Lusigny-sur-Barse.

Tourist Information: http://www.pnr-foret-orient.fr (in French)

Nearest vet: 22 Avenue Pierre Gomand, Lusigny-sur-Barse (GPS: 48° 15' 14.3994" N 4° 15' 33.8034" E). Tel: 03 25 46 02 53.

12

A5 (E17) Junction 22 Vendeuvre-sur-Barse

This small town is just on the edge of the Forêt d'Orient national park and, as it is well away from the more obviously touristic spots, the atmosphere here feels incredibly laid back and sleepy.

For visitors though, it means that you can get cheaper fuel and not expect to queue too long in the well-stocked supermarket. Look out for the display of tasty local produce at non-touristic prices.

Getting there

GPS: 48° 14' 25.4472" N 4° 28' 20.1426" E
8.6 km from A5

From junction 22 turn right at the T-junction signed D443, Bar s/Aube, Vendeuvre s/B. Carry straight on at a roundabout. Enter Vendeuvre-sur-Barse and at the crossroads continue straight on, signed Chaumont. Take the next right turn, signed Château Classe and continue, passing one car park on the left, to park in the ATAC supermarket car park on the right.

Return to A5 Junction 22

Exit the car park (past the fuel station) and at the T-junction turn right. Continue with the parkland on the left. Turn right at the sign for the A5 and at the next crossroads turn left. Continue following the signs to return to the A5.

Walk

The walk starts directly opposite the ATAC supermarket filling station on a large expanse of parkland behind the Château Classe.

The château stands on a 12th century site that was fought over, damaged, won, rebuilt and lost by a quick succession of owners in the 100 Years War. Even after that finished, somehow the castle never found a posh family who stayed there long enough to give it a proper name. The last owner, Boulon de Sarty, eventually donated the castle to the local municipality in 1978 and renovations have been going on since then. It's not open to the public 'for health and safety reasons'.

The grounds are a relaxing big open space that's great for a picnic, with plenty of space for children and dogs to run around on the grass.

Local info

Free parking. WC. Campervan access.

ATAC supermarket with a good selection of locally produced food specialities which we found were much cheaper than in the shops closer to the lakes. Mustards and cheeses are especially good value.

Refreshments: A couple café/bars in the town, and a good boulangerie.

Fuel station at the rear of the ATAC car park (pay at kiosk on exit), with discount prices.

Tourist Information: http://www.lacs-champagne.fr/en

Nearest vet: 1 Rue des Varennes, Vendeuvre sur Barse (GPS: 48° 14' 11.04" N 4° 27' 7.956" E). Tel: 03 25 41 38 92 (1.9 km).

13

A5 Junction 24 - Châteauvillain and Forêt de la Maison Renaud

The tiny village of Châteauvillain will give you a taste of life of feudal France and even today it's as if nothing has changed since medieval times. The village is surrounded by a huge deer park, with a number of trails to help you explore.

Dogs aren't allowed in the deer park, but there's a forest walk for them to enjoy before you get to the village.

Getting there

GPS: 48° 1' 25.1682" N 5° 1' 8.8356" E
6.3 km from A5

From junction 24 turn left signed Châteauvillain. Enter Richebourg and turn right D107, Châteauvillain at the sign. Exit Richebourg and continue ahead to enter woodland. Follow the road when it is chevroned to the right (ignoring a parking area on the left), and for the forest dog walk pull in to the next forest turning on the right. Stay on this road to reach Châteauvillain village.

Return to A5 Junction 24

From Châteauvillain return to Richebourg. Turn left when signed A5 and continue as signed to rejoin the A5.

Walk

1 Forêt de la Maison Renaud walk

If you have the time, this can be a major walk with almost limitless walking on firm tracks through this enormous piece of forestry. Don't get too carried away though - the delightful village of Châteauvillain is just a few kilometers further on, and well worth a visit.

We parked at the start of one section of a very long distance walking path marked by the two distinctive red and white bollards that indicate footpaths and leisure lanes.

From here, you can walk on the clear track that runs through the forest and it's an absolute delight. Dogs are fine off-lead and will adore the many scents of wildlife here.

2 Châteauvillain village and deer park

The village dates from around the 12th century, and still has the typical narrow streets and some astonishingly old buildings. Visitors are rare, and there are no coach parks or over-priced ice-creams. Instead, you can get a superb picnic from one of the diet-defying boulangerie/ patisseries and take a stroll into the deer park and around the village. Absolutely a taste of ‘real’ France, and completely lovely.

Local info

At forest: Free parking. Limited campervan access to pull-in.

In Châteauvillain: free parking, WC, pâtisseries, campervan access. Free entry to Châteauvillain Deer Park (no dogs).

Fuel: Intermarche supermarket with fuel and gas on the Route du Chatillon (D65) direction Bourdreville.

Nearest vet: Jean-Claude Guyot, 12 Route de Châtillon, Châteauvillain (GPS: 48° 1' 41.88" N 4° 54' 41.04" E). Tel: 03 25 32 94 74.

14

A31 (E17) Junction 6 - Auberive - Route Forestière de la Borde and Abbey

This is one of our favourite stops - with a fabulous off-lead forest walk for the dog and then, just a few miles down the road, there's a village with an excellent restaurant and an old Cistercian abbey with a medieval garden and heritage apple orchard to admire as well. If you're planning a long lunch in the restaurant you'll need to get the timing right and reserve in advance, but they will serve cold drinks as it's also a hotel.

Getting there

GPS: 47° 47' 27.24" N 5° 10' 34.8234" E
4.5 km from A31

From junction 6 turn left at the roundabout, signed Auberive. Pass through the village of Pierrefontaines, enter the forest and turn right to park at the side of a forest road between two footpath posts (these are red and white bollards). Continue on the same road to reach Auberive village.

Return to A31 Junction 6

Return to Pierrefontaines and continue ahead to rejoin the A31.

Walk

Forest walk
The footpath proper leaves the forest track just a meter or so after you start walking on it from the parking pull-in. It's clearly marked with the waymarks painted onto

trees, a yellow horizontal stripe above a red one. The route is that of the GR7 long distance footpath and this part of it can take enthusiastic walkers all 11kms to the village of Auberive.

The footpath can get quite muddy in wet weather, in which case the firm surface of the forest track is an easier option. This is also accessible to wheelchairs and buggies.

It's easy to get carried away here and walk for much longer than you might have intended - so don't forget to keep an eye on the time and turn round at your own half way point.

Local info

At the forest: free parking, campervan access.

In Auberive: free parking, campervan access. Pâtisserie just before you turn down the hill to the abbey, and chemist. The fine dining restaurant at the Auberge du Palais Abbatial deserves more than a short break and reservations for lunch are essential. Tel: 03 25 84 33 66. www.auberge-abbatiale.com

Nearest vet: Clinique Vétérinaire de la Citadelle, 40 Route de Dijon, Saints-Geosmes, Langres (GPS: 47° 50' 43.08" N 5° 19' 58.5114" E). Tel: 03 25 87 55 93 (15 km).

15

A31 (E17) Junction 4 - Arcelot

On a warm, sunny day a picnic by the river is perfect. Nothing happens in Arcelot, so dip your toes in the cooling water and relax!

Getting there

GPS: 47° 22' 5.8794" N 5° 11' 22.488" E
6.5 km from A31

From junction 4 take the D70 signed Arc-sur-Tille. Continue through Arc-sur-Tille and at the end of the village turn left, signed D34, Arcelot.

Enter Arcelot and turn left at the roundabout in front of the château. Turn right immediately after the bridge into the car park.

Return to A31 Junction 4

Turn left from the car park and cross the bridge. Turn right at the roundabout. Turn right onto the D70 and through Arc-sur-Tille to rejoin the motorway as signed.

Walk

The little hamlet of Arcelot is dominated by a château and just a few metres away from the imposing château gates you're in a world of peace and quiet, where picnic tables are set on a soft grassy clearing next to a bubbling river that's ideal for a dog dip, and a country farm lane running close to the river is ideal for a short stroll. On a baking hot day this is the ideal place for a short, undemanding stroll and a relaxed picnic under shade-giving trees.

For the stroll, take the obvious lane out of the car park (with the bridge behind you) and a gentle saunter will take you past cultivated fields in the direction of a farmhouse ahead. Dogs will enjoy nipping through the hedgerow into the soft grass on the other side. Children can safely spend hours playing in the river. If you look up, the trees host enormous round balls of mistletoe.

Local info

Free parking. Campervan access. Picnic tables.

SuperU supermarket with 24 hour fuel in Arc-sur-Tille.

Nearest vet: Cabinet Vétérinaire, 11 Route de Gray, Varois et Chaignot (GPS: 47° 20' 54.9594" N 5° 7' 46.524" E). Tel: 03 80 47 50 23 (5.4 km).

16

A31 (E17) Junction 4 - Base de Loisirs d'Arc-sur-Tille

An excellent family stop, in a park with fresh-water swimming and beaches. Summer weekends and school holidays can get very busy.

Getting there

GPS: 47° 20' 58.1994" N 5° 10' 11.712" E
1.6 km from A31

From junction 4 turn right, signed Arc-sur-Tille. At the next roundabout take exit 3, signed Base de Loisirs and squeeze through the height/width control into the car park. Park at the far end.

Note: height restriction of 1.7m and the width allows access only by a small family saloon car.

Return to A31 Junction 4
Leave the car park and turn right to return to the A31.

Walk

The walk here is in a set of leisure lakes, with good facilities and quite a lot going on. It's also a really easy place to get to, and just a few minutes away from the motorway exit.

From the far end of the car park follow signs to 'Plage' (beach) and walk through a tunnel under the road to emerge on the other side in front of an enormous lake.

As well as swimming, you'll find pedaloes to hire, water skiing and bike routes.

Dogs aren't allowed on the beach (unless it's well out of season and you have the place to yourself) but there's also a well tended and signed lakeside walk that goes on for miles.

Local info

Free parking, cars only.No campervan access. WC. Snacks and ice creams in summer. Lakeside beach, great for kids but not dogs.

SuperU supermarket with 24 hour fuel in Arc-sur-Tille (go straight on at the roundabout before turning into the park).

Nearest vet: Cabinet Vétérinaire, 11 Route de Gray, Varois et Chaignot (GPS: 47° 20' 54.9594" N 5° 7' 46.524" E). Tel: 03 80 47 50 23 (3.4 km).

17

A39 (E21) Junction 7.1 - Aire de Service de Jura

Magnificent motorway services, with spotless facilities and a fantastic choice of woodland trails. Not only that, there's a useful tourist information centre with bookshop, a shop for locally produced foods and local products that are perfect if you're in need of a treat or if you're good at forward planning for presents, and a choice of cafés/ restaurant with outdoor terraces, or picnic tables.

Getting there

GPS: 46° 46' 25.0854" N 5° 31' 20.2944" E

This Aire de Service is accessible from both north and southbound directions. Leave at junction 7.1 and follow signs to the Aire de Service, passing over a stylish viaduct to reach the car park.

Walk

This gets our 'best motorway services anywhere' trophy, without doubt!

Walk through the motorway services building on the gravel pathway and keep going, passing the children's play areas and expo cube to your left, until you reach an interpretation board. This is the start point for several marked trails that run over the fields and woodland.

The trails are well marked and easy to follow, and are perfect for drivers to unwind. Children can look for the wildlife marked on the interpretation boards, and dogs are fine off-lead.

Local info

Free parking. WC+disabled,

Restaurant, café and vending snacks. Children's play areas. Campervan and caravan access. Fuel. Expo cube with free exhibitions suitable for children. Picnic tables.

Tourist Information Centre and shop.
www.airedujura.com/en/presentation-aire-du-jura.html

18

A7 (E15) Junction 17- Mirmande

A gem of a village that's listed as one of France's prettiest villages; and it's easy to see why. Well worth a visit if you're staying in the area and a complete joy as a motorway break.

Getting there

GPS: 44° 41' 51.8676" N 4° 50' 11.0436" E
7.4 km from A7

From junction 17 take exit 1 at the roundabout, signed N7, Valence, Saulce. Continue on the N7 and enter Les Reys-de-Saulce. Turn right, signed D204A Mirmande, Marsanne. Pass through a sequence of bends to reach Mirmande.

Two routes are signed into the village - both will bring you to a car park half-way up the hill.

Return to A7 Junction 17

Return downhill and turn right. Retrace your route through Les Reys-de-Saulce, turning left at the T-junction to return to the A7.

Walk

The village is lovely and has won the accolade of being listed as one of France's prettiest. Several artists work and exhibit here, and studios may be visited without appointment. The church is often used as an exhibition space and is beautifully cool in summer.

Food is also a celebration. The locally produced honey is sensational and tastes of pure sunshine.

A walk around the village will take approximately 45 minutes, with a stunning view of the valley from the church.

Local info

Free parking.

Public WC (not disabled) concealed in a wall between two cafés.

Two café/restaurants at the lower fringe of the village near to the car park. Children and dogs are welcome at both and dog water bowls are provided.

Small general stores selling ice creams. Several artists' studios open to visitors.

Tourist Information: office open July/August. www.mirmande-tourisme.com (French only)

Nearest vet: Nicolas Cotton, Bances, Saulce-sur-Rhône (GPS: 44° 42' 51.8394" N 4° 47' 56.436" E). Tel: 04 75 42 93 19 (6.4 km).

19

A7 (E15) Junction 18 - Val des Nymphes and La Garde-Adhémar

Perched high on a hill overlooking the lavender fields is a charming and picturesque medieval walled citadel. La Garde-Adhémar is a popular spot to visit and it's a delight to wander through the narrow, shaded alleys before enjoying refreshments at one of the small outdoor restaurants near the square.

Getting there

GPS: 44° 23' 40.6566" N 4° 46' 32.1924" E
14.7 km from A7

From junction 18 take exit 3 at the roundabout signed N7, Valréas, Donzère, Pierrelatte. Continue for just over 1.5 km and at the next roundabout take exit 4 signed D133, Valréas.

After 3 km, turn right signed Les Granges-Gontardes. Continue ahead through the village and then turn left, signed D458, La Garde-Adhémar. There are two separate turnings very close to each other so if you miss the first one (easy to do), just continue to the next signed turn.

After a kilometre of bends enter the La Garde-Adhémar. To visit the village bear left and then park. For the walk at Val des Nymphes turn right as signed, pass a ruined chapel on the right and turn into the car park on the next bend.

Return to A7 Junction 18
Return to La Garde-Adhémar and turn left at the junction to follow the bendy road back to the D458. Turn right.

At the junction with the D541 turn left, signed Donzère. Enter the town and at the roundabout turn right, N7. Follow the motorway signs to rejoin the A7.

Walk

Val de Nymphes
A perfect walking place, with a selection of routes ranging from a 20 minute stroll to several hours of purposeful hiking. The walks are ideal for dogs, and just as enjoyable for people. The vegetation lets you know that you're in the south, with aromatic herbs and heat-hardy trees giving some shade over the sandy paths.

Before you start your walk, do take a look at the ruined chapel which was built on top of a much earlier site of mysterious local water deities.

No one could complain about lack of choice for a walk here. I don't think I've seen a single wooden post with so many footpath markers.

Just a short drive away is the charming medieval Provençale village of La Garde-Adhémar. The shady central square hosts a number of small restaurants and a charming tea salon, all with outdoor tables.

Local info

Val des Nymphes: Free parking, campervan access.

La Garde-Adhémar: Free parking. Campervan access, with care. Several small restaurant/cafés and tea garden - dogs welcome at the outside tables.

If you need Internet access, head to the 'Emaillerie' just off the main square and near the school.

Tourist Information Office: www.la-garde-adhemar-ot.org/english/

Nearest vet: Clinique Vétérinaire, 49 Avenue Maréchal de Lattre de Tassigny, Pierrelatte (GPS: 44° 23' 7.4394" N 4° 41' 50.5674" E). Tel: 04 75 04 00 03 (8.4 km).

20

A7 (E15) Junction 19 - Suze-la-Rousse Castle

A medieval castle in excellent condition, surrounded by a hunting forest makes a great place for a break. On a clear day the view from the castle is stunning.

Getting there

GPS: 44° 17' 23.0352" N 4° 50' 11.187" E
10 km from A7

From junction 19 take exit 4 at the roundabout, signed D8, Suze, Nyons. At the junction with the D994, turn left, signed Suze, Nyons. Enter Suze-la-Rousse and turn left signed Gendarmerie, Château. Continue following the signs for the château to reach the car park at the top of the hill.

Return to A7 Junction 19

Return to the main road and turn right and follow the signs for the A7. Continue following the signs to return to junction 19 of the A7.

Walk

The forest trails start from the castle car park and run through the dark-barked pine trees for several miles. An information board with a plan of the forest trails is between the car park and the castle entrance. The routes are short enough to complete in 30-40 minutes, and paths are easy to follow.

We also tried walking around the castle - but this doesn't work at all, although the students from the renowned wine university that nestles in the castle ramparts are a very friendly bunch.

The town below the castle is tiny, and there isn't a huge amount going on there although you will find a few cafés and shops.

Local info

Free parking. Campervan access. Shops in the town, including a chemist and several boulangerie and pâtisserie for snacks, picnic supplies, or just cakes.

Fuel: Garage Labrouve on the right as you approach the town (limited opening hours).

Tourist Information Office: 445, Avenue des Côtes du Rhône, Suze-la-Rousse.
www.ot-suze-la-rousse.fr/contact.html

Nearest vet: Clinique Vétérinaire de Bollène Ecluse, Avenue Jean Moulin, Bollène (GPS: 44° 18' 25.5594" N 4° 44' 50.424" E). Tel: 04 90 30 07 37 (13.7 km).

21

A7 (E15) Junction 21 - Orange

What's so fantastic about the Roman theatre in Orange is that it doesn't take itself too seriously, and you really get the feeling that this is still a place where people go to be entertained and have a laugh. Just like it would have been way back in Roman times. If you're introducing children to the idea of the Romans, this is a good place to start because the theatre is still in use, and isn't just another boring ruin.

Getting there

GPS: 44° 8' 2.1798" N 4° 48' 41.8896" E
2.1 km from A7

Comprehensively signed from the A7.

From junction 21 take exit 2 at the roundabout, signed D17, Centre Ville. Continue ahead at the next roundabout, and at the following roundabout take exit 1, signed Avignon, Nîmes. Bear right at the end and follow the signs for Avignon, Theatre Antique. Drive past the theatre and continue ahead to reach a car park on the right hand side.

Return to A7 Junction 21
Turn right from the car park, then left at the junction. Continue ahead, following signs to the A7. At the roundabout, take exit 1 signed A7. Continue to the A7 as signed.

Walk

To make the most of your visit, pick up an audio-guide from the ticket office as you enter and this will take you around the theatre with an entertaining and informative commentary in English. If you're lucky you may also see performers rehearsing on the stage.

The theatre shop sells souvenirs and a tasty selection of fresh locally-made nougat.

Dogs can go everywhere in the theatre, and the town is generally very dog-friendly.

Local info

Parking - there are several large P&D car parks near the theatre which are well-signed from every direction. Campervan access.

Plenty of restaurants and cafés near the theatre, as well as a mix of tourist and useful shops.

Entry charges to the theatre include the nearby museum too; larger dogs are not welcome in the museum.

Tourist Information Office: 5 cours Aristide Briand, Orange. www.otorange.fr

Fuel: Intermarché supermarket with fuel on the D17, Avenue Charles de Gaulle.

Nearest vet: Dr Claude Gantet, 825 Boulevard Edouard Daladier, Orange (GPS: 44° 8' 4.2" N 4° 48' 44.4954" E). Tel: 04 90 34 10 31.

22

A7 (E714) Junction 22 - Châteauneuf du Pape

The village of Châteauneuf du Pape is unsurprisingly devoted to wine: tasting, drinking and selling it. Just as fascinating is the view of the vines stretching off into the distance from the window of a romantic ruined tower, and a leg stretch through the small medieval village below.

Getting there

GPS: 44° 3' 29.3574" N 4° 49' 44.8464" E
9 km from A7

From junction 22 take exit 1 signed La Gironde. Drive over the A7 and take the 1st left turn (there are small signs to restaurants in Châteauneuf du Pape). Continue ahead through the vineyards and turn right at the main road. At the roundabout, take exit 3 signed D68 Châteauneuf du Pape, and continue straight (exit 1) at the next roundabout. Turn left through a gap in the stone wall and continue ahead to reach a large car park.

Return to A7 Junction 22

Exit the car park and turn right. At the roundabout take exit 2, signed Orange. Continue straight at the next roundabout. Turn right onto the narrow lane signed Domaine de Marcoux (5.5 T weight limit) and continue ahead to return to rejoin the A7.

Walk

By this stage of the A7 you will already have driven through the vineyards of the champagne production region and its discreetly affluent villages. If you've stopped to try and find a bargain, then you'll already know that prices for a bottle of bubbly with a recognisable name are likely to be cheaper in your local supermarket at home.

Here, though, is the chance to try some fine wines and also experience some of the history and culture which make the labels something a bit special. And of course the children and dog can come too.

The large car park overlooking the village and surrounding fields of bushy vines is the start point. And as this area is famed for its long, hot sunny days then most dogs will be quite happy with a short snuffle in the fields next to the car park before joining you in an exploration of the cooler palace ruins and restaurants/bars of the village lower down the slope.

The 14th century palace isn't hugely exciting as a ruin but does have an amazing ability to turn the hot hairdryer-like breeze into a cool and refreshing fan effect when you sit by the windows. There's probably some serious engineering science at work here, and the builders of the 'Pope's new castle' certainly knew what they were about. The views are also outstanding, with the great plain of the Rhône laid out beneath you as a shimmering counterpane of foliage. Entry is free.

The walk continues down into the village where you'll find several bar/restaurants, the most popular seems to be the *Verger des Papes* and its related wine tasting *'cave'*. Children and dogs are welcome, and are given water rather than wine.

Local info

Free parking. WC in village. Campervan access.

Tourist Information Office: Place du Portail, Châteauneuf-du-Pape

www.pays-provence.fr/chateauneuf_du_pape_tourisme.html

Nearest vet: Sandrine Lebon, 22 Avenue de la Gare, Bédarrides (GPS: 44° 2' 27.5994" N 4° 53' 36.78" E). Tel: 04 90 33 23 31 (8 km).

23

A7 Junction 25 - Cavaillon

The big deal here is melons. Cavaillon is France's melon capital with all sorts of events, celebrations and melon competitions in August.

The only serious nod to tourism is a large Roman arch in front of the Tourist Office, which is a very handy landmark but otherwise looks like an archway in need of some chariots.

Getting there

GPS: 43° 49' 59.8938" N 5° 1' 52.3272" E
3.4 km from A7

From junction 25 take the right hand lane signed Cavaillon to merge with the D99. Drive over the river and at the roundabout take exit 4 signed Carpentras, Avignon. At the next roundabout take exit 1 to enter Cavaillon, and at the following roundabout take exit 1 signed Centre Ville. Drive past the park on the left hand side and, after the hedge ends, turn left (unsigned). Drive towards the mountain and turn left at the T-junction onto a no through road. Turn right at the end to reach the parking area.

Return to A7 Junction 25

Return the same way, taking the 1st left, then the 1st right. At the T-junction turn right and at the roundabout take exit 2, signed A7. The A7 is clearly signed from this point.

Walk

There are two walks here.

The first walk is a worthy clamber up to the top of the Mont St Jacques and a fine panoramic view over the Luberon area. The walk starts from the flight of steps next to the Tourism Office, and behind the Roman arch. On a cool and crisp day the view is rewarding, and the uphill is worth doing.

The second walk takes you on a linear route under overhanging cliffs below Mont St Jacques on a gentle path with paw-cooling grass for dogs. It's not very long, and makes for an ideal stroll before going into the town and investigating the sights there.

Cavaillon is a completely un-special town, and that is a big part of its charm. You'll find very reasonably priced cafés and restaurants and a good selection of general and specialist food shops.

Local info

Some free parking or on-street P&D. WC by Tourist Information Office. Campervan *aire* and parking.

Food enthusiasts should head for the fine cheese shop - 'Fromagerie des Alpes' (67 rue Raspail, close to the *Mairie*), and look out for locally produced olive oil too. Wine tasting and sales of Luberon wine can be found in one of the many '*Caves*' in the area.

Fuel: TOTAL fuel station on the D99, Avenue de Verdun.

Tourist Information Office: Place François Tourel, Cavaillon www.cavaillon-luberon.com (French only)

Nearest vet: Robert Agnès, 50 Boulevard Fleury Mitifiot, Cavaillon (GPS: 43° 50' 8.52" N 5° 2' 29.0034" E). Tel: 04 90 78 00 33.

24

A7 (E714) Junction 26 - Mallemort

The walk here is particularly rewarding for bridge enthusiasts as the main feature is the last surviving 19th century wooden suspension bridge in France.

Getting there

GPS: 43° 44' 24.651" N 5° 10' 31.1226" E
8.6 km from A7

From exit 26 keep in the left hand lane after the péage, following the sign for Six-en-P, Nice. At the roundabout turn left, signed Aix-en-P, Mallemort. Continue ahead for 5.5 km. At the roundabout take exit 3 signed D23 Mallemort. Continue to the next roundabout and take exit 3 signed D23, Mérindol, Cavaillon. Drive over the river (the old bridge can be seen to the left) and take the 1st left turn to enter the car park.

Return to A7 Junction 26

Turn right out of the car park, continue over the bridge and at the roundabout take exit 2 signed Lamanon, Salon. At the next roundabout, take exit 1 signed A7 and continue to follow the blue autoroute signs to return to the A7.

Walk

The walk here starts underneath a fascinating old wooden suspension bridge. The first bridge here was constructed in around 1845, and was then rebuilt four times after floods washed it away every 4 years or so between 1872 and 1886. The German army later damaged it again in 1940 - so it's a miracle that there's anything left at all. It's the only bridge of its era left standing. You can't get onto the bridge, but it's nevertheless an extraordinary sight.

This is a great spot for a proper walk for the dog - and the owners of the big slobbery Cane Corsos in the photo told us that it was one of the best off-lead spaces in the area.

From the car park, take the obvious sandy path away from the cars and then follow the path as it generally follows the course of the river Durance. There are little paths off to the side, and these meet up with the main path sooner or later.

This is a linear walk, so simply reverse the route to return to the bridge when you're ready.

Local info

Free parking. Campervan access. Picnic tables at the start of the walk.

Shops, several bakeries and cafés in the village of Mallemort. And a ruined castle with a good view at the top of the village.

TOTAL fuel station at the N7/D23 roundabout.

Tourist Information Office: 7 avenue des Frères Roqueplan, Mallemort (on the hill)
http://www.mallemortdeprovence.com/vis_index.php

Nearest vet: Clinique vétérinaire, 20 Avenue Joliot Curie, Mallemort (GPS: 43° 43' 41.1594" N 5° 10' 40.764" E). Tel: 04 90 59 46 00.

25

A55 Junction 13 - Martigues Marina

Slightly to the west of Marseilles, Martigues is a useful place for a quiet overnight stay if you’re catching a ferry from Marseilles.

Getting there

GPS: 43° 24' 22.6038" N 5° 2' 56.2092" E
1.4 km from A55

From junction 13 take exit 1 signed Martigues-Ferrières. Take the left hand lane and follow the sign for Ferrières, Centre Ville. Continue ahead at a roundabout and turn right signed Centre Ville, Hôtel de Ville. At the roundabout by the Hôtel de Ville/Tourist Information Office park in one of the marked bays.

Return to A55 Junction 13

From the roundabout by the Hôtel de Ville, follow the blue autoroute sign. The way back to the A55 is clearly marked with blue autoroute signs.

Walk

Once a lair for marauding pirates this small town is now one of the largest marinas for yachts and pleasure boats in the Med.

Behind the Tourist Info office is an expanse of green space with access to the protected waters of the harbour inlet. It's ideal for a cooling doggie dip and quiet enough to almost count as a private beach.

After that, a stroll alongside the marina gives you a chance to admire some dream yachts on the way into the town for a meal or drink at one of the many small restaurants and cafés that fringe the waterside. The speciality here is shellfish, unsurprisingly. There's no fuss about dogs and most of the dining tables are outside.

The town is in three parts, divided by canals, and if you want to explore thoroughly walking guides are available from the Tourist Office.

Remember to protect yourself against mosquitoes in the evening; this is the eastern fringe of the Camargue where scientists swarm to study the many varieties of the evil insect.

Local info

Free parking. Campervan access. WC. Restaurants, cafés and shops in Martigues. Tourist Information Office: Route Départementale, Pt de L Hotel de ville, Martigues http://www.martigues-tourisme.com

Nearest vet: Clinique Vétérinaire Sainte Anne, 1 Allée Dominique Ingres, Martigues (GPS: 43° 23' 57.12" N 5° 3' 49.032" E). Tel: 04 42 07 07 49.

I hope you've enjoyed using the walks in this book. If you'd like to send your feedback direct to the author, and find out about new motorway walks, you can contact me through www.drivingwithdogs.co.uk

More motorway guides by Lezli Rees:

In France

20 Short Walks near Calais, France for drivers, families and dogs
ISBN 978-0-9927197-0-8 £7.99 (RRP)
E-book: 978-0-9927197-1-5

In UK

Walking the Dog – motorway walks for drivers and dogs RAC publications.
ISBN 978-1845841027 £4.99 (RRP)
App also available, search 'Walking the Dog' in App Stores

Coming soon for 2015

Drive Right in France, from Calais/Cherbourg to Biarritz and Calais to Perpignan Walks for drivers,

families and dogs within 10km autoroute exits on popular routes.
For more info and to pre-order please e-mail via www.drivingwithdogs.co.uk

Notes